Better Homes and Gardens.

Fast-Fixin' Kids' Recipes

Our seal assures you that every recipe in *Fast-Fixin' Kids' Recipes*
has been tested in the Better Homes and Gardens® Test Kitchen.
This means that each recipe is practical and reliable,
and meets our high standards of taste appeal.

BETTER HOMES AND GARDENS® BOOKS

Editor: Gerald M. Knox
Art Director: Ernest Shelton
Managing Editor: David A. Kirchner
Editorial Project Managers: James D. Blume, Marsha Jahns,
    Rosanne Weber Mattson, Mary Helen Schiltz

Department Head, Cook Books: Sharyl Heiken
Associate Department Heads: Sandra Granseth,
    Rosemary C. Hutchinson, Elizabeth Woolever
Senior Food Editors: Julia Malloy, Marcia Stanley,
    Joyce Trollope
Associate Food Editors: Linda Henry, Mary Major,
    Diana McMillen, Mary Jo Plutt, Martha Schiel,
    Linda Foley Woodrum
Test Kitchen: Director, Sharon Stilwell; Photo Studio Director,
    Janet Herwig; Home Economists: Jean Brekke, Kay Cargill,
    Marilyn Cornelius, Jennifer Darling, Maryellyn Krantz,
    Lynelle Munn, Dianna Nolin, Marge Steenson

Associate Art Directors: Linda Ford Vermie, Neoma Thomas,
    Randall Yontz
Assistant Art Directors: Lynda Haupert, Harijs Priekulis,
    Tom Wegner
Graphic Designers: Mary Schlueter Bendgen, Mike Burns,
    Brian Wignall
Art Production: Director, John Berg; Associate, Joe Heuer;
    Office Manager, Michaela Lester

President, Book Group: Fred Stines
Vice President, General Manager: Jeramy Lanigan
Vice President, Retail Marketing: Jamie L. Martin
Vice President, Administrative Services: Rick Rundall

BETTER HOMES AND GARDENS® MAGAZINE
President, Magazine Group: James A. Autry
Vice President, Editorial Director: Doris Eby
Executive Director, Editorial Services: Duane L. Gregg
Food and Nutrition Editor: Nancy Byal

MEREDITH CORPORATE OFFICERS
Chairman of the Board: E.T. Meredith III
President: Robert A. Burnett
Executive Vice President: Jack D. Rehm

FAST-FIXIN' KIDS' RECIPES

Editor: Diana McMillen
Editorial Project Manager: Marsha Jahns
Graphic Designers: Brenda Cort, Lynda Haupert
Electronic Text Processor: Paula Forest
Food Stylists: Janet Herwig, Judy Tills
Contributing Photographers: Ron Crofoot, Michael Jensen,
    Scott Little

On the cover: *Micro Burger*
(see recipe, page 47)

Contents

Fitting the Mealtime Puzzle Together

What's for dinner? *Fast-Fixin' Kids' Recipes* gives you the answer—dozens of easy-does-it recipes that were tasted by a panel of honest-to-gosh kids (see photos, pages 60 and 61) to ensure that your kids will like the recipes, too.

But best of all, we designed the recipes so parents can make them *fast*. Most recipes go together in less than 30 minutes. The extra-fast ones (less than 15 minutes) are marked for easy reference.

Personal Pizza
(see recipe, page 36)

Accordion Sandwiches

Total Time: 30 minutes

1	**12- to 14-inch loaf Italian *or* French bread**
¼	**cup mayonnaise *or* salad dressing**
1	**tablespoon Italian salad dressing**
1	**tablespoon grated Parmesan cheese**

● Preheat the oven to 375°. Cut bread into 16 slices, cutting to, but not through, the bottom crust. In a small bowl stir together mayonnaise or salad dressing, Italian salad dressing, and Parmesan.

2	**2½-ounce packages very thinly sliced chicken *or* turkey**
1	**2½-ounce package very thinly sliced ham**
1	**6-ounce package Monterey Jack *or* cheddar cheese slices**

● Tuck chicken or turkey, ham, and cheese slices between every other bread slice. Place a well-rounded teaspoon of mayonnaise mixture in the slits with the meat, spreading slightly. (If the loaf breaks apart, press a piece of foil around the bottom of the loaf.)

● Place on a baking sheet. Bake loaf in the 375° oven about 15 minutes or till hot. Makes 8 servings.

When you're serving a family of four, save half the sandwich for later. Wrap the unbaked half in foil and freeze. To serve, bake the frozen wrapped loaf in a 350° oven for 25 minutes. Unwrap top of loaf. Bake for 5 to 10 minutes more or till top is crisp and sandwich is heated through.

Hamburger In Disguise

Total Time: 25 minutes

1	**pound ground beef**
½	**teaspoon seasoned salt**
4	**slices American *or* Swiss cheese (optional)**

● Preheat the broiler. Mix together the meat and seasoned salt. Shape into 4 logs, 6 to 7 inches long. Place on the rack of an unheated broiler pan. Broil 3 to 4 inches from the heat about 10 minutes or till done, turning once. If desired, top with the cheese slices.

4	**hot dog buns, split** **Pickle relish (optional)** **Prepared mustard (optional)** **Catsup (optional)**

● Serve on buns with relish, mustard, and catsup, if desired. Makes 4 servings.

What's the disguise? It's a hamburger shaped like a hot dog and served in a hot dog bun.

It's Italian! Sausage Sandwich

Total Time: 30 minutes

¾ **pound bulk Italian sausage** *or* **ground beef**
1 **16-ounce jar spaghetti sauce**
½ **cup sliced pitted ripe olives**

● Preheat the oven to 375°. In a skillet brown sausage. Drain off fat. Stir in sauce and olives. Heat through.

If you know French rolls are too tough for your child to chew, serve the sandwich on hamburger or hot dog buns.

4 **French-style rolls**
4 **slices mozzarella cheese (6 ounces)**

● Split rolls lengthwise without cutting through opposite side. Hollow out buns slightly. Halve cheese slices lengthwise. Place a piece of cheese on bottom half of each roll. Divide meat mixture evenly among the 4 rolls. Place another cheese slice half atop meat. Close rolls.

● Wrap each sandwich in foil and seal. Place on a baking sheet. Bake wrapped sandwiches in the 375° oven for 15 minutes. Unwrap and serve. Serves 4.

Some of our young testers only had room for half a sandwich.

Reuben Submarine

Total Time: 20 minutes

1 **8-ounce loaf unsliced French bread, halved lengthwise**
¼ **cup mayonnaise** *or* **salad dressing**
1 **tablespoon prepared mustard**
8 **ounces process Swiss cheese slices, halved diagonally**

● Preheat the oven to 425°. Place bread halves in a 15½x10½x1-inch baking pan. Stir together mayonnaise and mustard. Spread on cut surface of bread. Top with cheese triangles.

Although this sandwich never goes under water like a real submarine, it'll go down easy when you eat it for lunch or dinner.

½ **pound thinly sliced corned beef, chicken,** *or* **other deli meat, cut into bite-size strips**
1 **8-ounce can sauerkraut, rinsed and well drained**

● In a medium mixing bowl toss together meat and sauerkraut.

● Divide meat mixture evenly between bread halves in baking pan. Bake, uncovered, in the 425° oven for 5 to 10 minutes or till warm and cheese begins to melt. Serve the sandwiches open face. Makes 4 to 6 servings.

Rolled-Up Pickle Steak

Total Time: 25 minutes

4 beef cubed steaks (4 ounces each) ½ of an 8-ounce container soft-style cream cheese Prepared mustard (optional) 2 whole dill *or* sweet pickles (3 to 4 inches long), halved	● Spread 1 side of each steak with cream cheese and lightly with mustard, if desired. Roll up each steak around a pickle half (*see photo, below*). Trim each pickle to fit and secure with wooden toothpicks, if necessary.	**If dill is your family's pickle preference, choose from regular or garlic pickle varieties.**
1 tablespoon cooking oil	● Preheat a large skillet over medium heat. Add oil. Cook beef rolls in hot oil for 10 to 12 minutes or till no pink remains, turning occasionally. Transfer meat to a serving platter.	
Catsup	● Serve meat rolls with catsup. Serves 4.	

Place a halved pickle atop steak with cream cheese and mustard. Roll up the steak around the pickle. Use a wooden toothpick to secure steak, if necessary.

Pan-Style Taco

Total Time: 30 minutes

Corn muffin mix forms the crust of a taco built in a baking dish.

Nonstick spray coating *or* shortening
1 7- *or* 8½-ounce package corn muffin mix

● Preheat the oven to 400°. Spray a 10x6x2-inch baking dish with nonstick spray coating or grease with shortening. Prepare corn muffin mix according to package directions. Spread corn muffin batter evenly in prepared dish. Bake in the 400° oven for 18 to 20 minutes or till corn-muffin layer is done.

¾ pound ground beef *or* pork
1 cup mild taco sauce
½ cup shredded cheddar cheese (2 ounces)

● Meanwhile, in a medium skillet brown meat. Drain fat. Stir in taco sauce. Heat through. Spoon over muffin layer in baking dish. Sprinkle cheese over meat. Return to oven. Bake for 1 to 2 minutes more or till cheese melts.

1 cup shredded iceberg lettuce
Taco sauce *or* salsa (optional)

● Serve topped with lettuce and additional taco sauce or salsa, if desired. Makes 6 servings.

Take-Along Hot Dogs

For your next family-style potluck take a crockery cooker full of frankfurters. Let participants serve themselves and watch the franks get gobbled up.

Start at home by heating the frankfurters in water. Using tongs, transfer franks to the crockery cooker. Pour in 2 to 3 inches of hot water.

Transport your filled crockery cooker to the location of the gathering. Plug it in and set it on high. Don't forget to bring along tongs to grab the franks. Have hot dog buns and condiments (catsup, mustard, relish, and more) next to the cooker.

Jumbo Meatballs With Sauce

Total Time: 40 minutes

1	beaten egg
¼	cup fine dry bread crumbs
½	pound ground fully cooked ham
½	pound ground pork *or* ground raw turkey

● Preheat the oven to 400°. In a medium bowl stir together the egg and bread crumbs. Add ground ham and pork. Mix well. Shape into 8 large meatballs. Arrange meatballs in a shallow baking pan. Bake in the 400° oven for 20 to 25 minutes or till done. Drain fat.

1	7½-ounce can semicondensed mushroom soup
1	cup frozen peas
¼	cup milk
¼	cup dairy sour cream Hot cooked noodles (optional)

● In a small saucepan heat together the mushroom soup, frozen peas, milk, and sour cream till mixture is heated through. Serve over hot meatballs and noodles, if desired. Makes 4 servings.

All of the kid tasters liked these meatballs. One group insisted on finishing every last meatball, they liked them so much.

Mac and Cheese Special

Total Time: 20 minutes

1	7½-, 12-, *or* 14-ounce package macaroni and cheese dinner mix

● Prepare mix according to package directions, *except* start cooking the pasta with *hot* water.

½	cup sour cream and buttermilk dip, sour cream dip with toasted onion, *or* sour cream dip with chives
8	ounces frankfurters (4 or 5), cut lengthwise and sliced ½ inch thick

● Stir in dip, then frankfurters. Heat through. Makes 4 to 6 servings.

If you have an older home and are concerned about the lead content of your hot tap water, take a few extra minutes to start cooking the pasta with cold water.

Chili Challenge

When chili madness strikes your family, choose one of the tasty specialties below. Each kid-approved recipe is guaranteed to stifle dinnertime yawns.

Idaho Chili Stew
(see recipe, page 14)

Hawaiian Chili
(see recipe, page 15)

Texas Chili
(see recipe, page 14)

Cincinnati Chili
(see recipe, page 15)

EXTRA FAST

Total Time: 15 minutes

Texas Chili

Pictured on pages 12 and 13.

2 cups leftover cooked roast beef, cut into small cubes, *or* cooked ground beef (about 10 ounces)
1 12-ounce jar salsa
½ cup water
1 teaspoon beef bouillon granules
1 teaspoon chili powder
½ teaspoon ground cumin

● In a medium saucepan combine meat, salsa, water, bouillon granules, chili powder, and cumin. Bring to boiling. Reduce heat. Simmer mixture, covered, about 10 minutes.

Texas chili pros refuse to mix the chili meat with the chili beans. If you're not a chili purist and want to avoid washing a second saucepan, mix the drained beans with the meat and heat through.

1 15-ounce can pinto beans
Fresh chili peppers *or* sweet pickles (optional)
Texas toast (optional)

● Meanwhile, in a small saucepan heat *undrained* beans. Drain. Serve meat and beans with chili peppers or sweet pickles and Texas toast, if desired. Serves 4.

Idaho Chili Stew

Total Time: 45 minutes

Pictured on pages 12 and 13.

2 cups tomato juice
1 15-ounce can garbanzo beans
1 cup water
1 medium potato, peeled and chopped
½ cup lentils, rinsed and drained
1 carrot, cut into 1-inch strips *or* sliced
1 tablespoon cooked bacon pieces
1 tablespoon minced dried onion
2 teaspoons chili powder
1 teaspoon instant beef bouillon granules

● In a large saucepan combine tomato juice, *undrained* garbanzo beans, water, potato, lentils, carrot, bacon pieces, onion, chili powder, and the bouillon granules. Bring to boiling. Reduce heat. Cover and simmer about 30 minutes or till lentils are tender.

Potatoes and lentils from Idaho spark up this yummy meatless main dish. If your family loves meat in chili, stir in ½ pound of any cubed cooked meat.

Dairy sour cream *or* shredded cheddar cheese
Snipped chives (optional)
Tortilla chips (optional)

● Spoon into bowls. Top with sour cream or cheese and sprinkle with snipped chives, if desired. Serve with tortilla chips, if desired. Makes 4 servings.

Cincinnati-Style Chili

Total Time: 30 minutes

Pictured on pages 12 and 13.

1	**pound ground beef**
1	**tablespoon minced dried onion**
1	**15½-ounce can kidney beans, drained**
1	**8-ounce can tomato sauce**
½	**cup beef broth**
1	**tablespoon chili powder**
1	**tablespoon semisweet chocolate pieces**
1	**tablespoon vinegar**
2	**teaspoons pumpkin pie spice**
½	**teaspoon salt**

● In a medium saucepan cook beef and onion till beef is brown. Drain fat. Stir in beans, tomato sauce, beef broth, chili powder, chocolate, vinegar, pumpkin pie spice, and salt. Bring to boiling. Reduce heat. Cover; simmer about 15 minutes.

What's different about this chili? Chocolate and pumpkin pie spice head the list. Then it's served over noodles. Our kid tasters noticed the difference and rated the chili A+.

8	**ounces fettuccine, broken into 4-inch lengths, *or* 8 ounces egg noodles**

● Meanwhile, cook pasta according to package directions.

	Sliced onion (optional)
2	**cups shredded cheddar cheese**

● To serve, divide pasta among 4 plates. Make a well in the center of each. Top with meat sauce and sliced onion, if desired; then cheese. Makes 4 servings.

Hawaiian Chili

Total Time: 20 minutes

Pictured on pages 12 and 13.

1	**pound ground pork *or* beef**
1	**14½-ounce can tomatoes, cut up**
1	**8-ounce can red kidney beans, drained**
1	**8-ounce can tomato sauce**
2	**tablespoons soy sauce**
1	**tablespoon chili powder**
1	**teaspoon minced dried onion**

● In a 3-quart saucepan brown ground pork or beef. Drain fat. Stir in *undrained* tomatoes, kidney beans, tomato sauce, soy sauce, chili powder, and dried onion. Bring to boiling. Reduce heat and simmer chili mixture, uncovered, about 10 minutes.

Chris, one of our kid tasters, said this island-style chili reminded him of Chinese take-out.

1½	**cups water**
1½	**cups quick-cooking rice**

● Meanwhile, in a small saucepan bring water to boiling. Stir in rice. Remove from heat and let stand for 5 minutes.

	Chow mein noodles (optional)
	Pineapple slices (optional)
	Seedless grapes (optional)

● Spoon rice onto 4 plates. Spoon chili over rice. Top with chow mein noodles, if desired. Serve with pineapple slices and grapes, if desired. Makes 4 servings.

Puff the Magic Pancake

Total Time: 30 minutes

4 beaten eggs
⅔ cup all-purpose flour
⅔ cup milk

● Grease a 10-inch ovenproof skillet with shortening. Place in the oven. Preheat the oven to 400° (about 10 minutes). Meanwhile, in a medium mixing bowl beat together the eggs, all-purpose flour, and milk till smooth. Pour into the hot skillet (see photo below).

Eggs make this puff rise. Let your child watch you put the batter together. When it's done, call him or her to the kitchen to see the amazing puff come from the oven.

1 cup finely shredded Swiss, cheddar, *or* Monterey Jack cheese (4 ounces)
2 tablespoons cooked bacon pieces

● Bake in the 400° oven about 20 minutes or till pancake is puffed and golden. Sprinkle with cheese, then bacon pieces. Cut into wedges to serve. Serves 4.

Preheating the skillet allows the batter to start cooking the minute you pour it into the pan. Then, as the batter bakes in the oven, it puffs magically.

EXTRA FAST

Total Time: 15 minutes

Broiled Peanut Butter Sandwich

8 **slices white, whole wheat, or cinnamon-raisin bread** ½ **to ⅔ cup creamy or chunky-style peanut butter** ⅓ **cup desired jelly, jam, or marmalade**	● Preheat the broiler. Spread *half* of the bread slices with peanut butter, then add the desired jelly, jam, or marmalade. Top with remaining bread slices.
	● Broil 4 inches from the heat for 1 to 2 minutes or till toasted. Turn and broil for 1 to 2 minutes more. Serves 4.
	Creamy Broiled Peanut Butter Sandwich: Prepare as above, *except* substitute ⅓ cup soft-style *cream cheese* mixed with 1 tablespoon *honey* for the jelly, jam, or marmalade.
	Carrot-Raisin Broiled Peanut Butter Sandwich: Prepare as above, *except* substitute a combination of ¼ cup *raisins* and ¼ cup shredded *carrot* for the jelly, jam, or marmalade.

We took every kid's favorite—a peanut butter sandwich—added a special topper, and broiled it for a tasty treat. (Even parents will love it!)

EXTRA FAST

Total Time: 15 minutes

Ready-Right-Now Sloppy Joes

1 **pound ground beef, pork, or raw turkey**	● In a large skillet brown ground beef, pork, or turkey. Drain fat.
1 **8-ounce can tomato sauce** ⅓ **cup bottled barbecue sauce** 1 **teaspoon minced dried onion**	● Stir in tomato sauce, barbecue sauce, and onion. Bring to boiling. Remove from heat.
6 **hamburger buns, split**	● Spoon into buns. Makes 6 servings.

It's fast, it's easy, and it's great. You can't miss.

The Salad Bar

Total Time: 20 minutes

1 cup Vegetables/Fruits
1½ cups Meats/Fish
4 ounces Cheeses
4 cups torn iceberg lettuce

● In a large salad bowl combine your choices from Vegetables/Fruits, Meats/Fish, and Cheeses with the lettuce.

Set out the salad options for dinner and let your youngsters create their own salads. Serve with just-baked bread made from refrigerated French or whole wheat bread dough.

Desired bottled salad dressing
1 Topping

● Pour salad dressing over mixture. Toss lightly to coat. Sprinkle with your choice of Topping. Makes 3 or 4 main-dish servings.

VEGETABLES/FRUITS:

Shredded carrot
Whole mushrooms, halved or quartered
Tomato wedges
Canned mandarin orange sections
Canned pineapple chunks
Seedless red *or* green grapes

MEATS/FISH:

1 6- or 6½-ounce can of tuna, chicken, *or* ham, drained and flaked
1 7½-ounce can boneless, skinless salmon, drained and flaked
Sliced lunch meats cut into bite-size strips
Leftover meat cut into bite-size pieces

CHEESES:

Preshredded cheddar, mozzarella, *or* Swiss cheese
Sliced cheese cut into strips

TOPPINGS:

Sliced pitted ripe olives
Peanuts
Sunflower nuts
Cooked bacon pieces
Croutons
Grated Parmesan cheese
Crushed canned French-fried onions
Raisins
Deli hard-cooked eggs, sliced *or* chopped

Eggs and More Eggs

The egg is Mother Nature's gift to busy cooks. It cooks fast, stores well, and comes in a nifty package. Sample the egg's versatility in these three recipes.

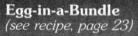

Egg-in-a-Bundle
(see recipe, page 23)

Eggs 'n' Tators
(see recipe, page 22)

Ham-It-Up Eggwiches
(see recipe, page 22)

Ham-It-Up Eggwiches

Total Time: 20 minutes

Pictured on pages 20 and 21.

2 tablespoons margarine *or* butter	● In a 10-inch skillet melt margarine or butter. Meanwhile, in a bowl beat together eggs and milk. Stir in ham. Pour egg mixture into skillet. Cook, without stirring, over medium heat till mixture begins to set on the bottom and around the edges. Using a large spoon or spatula, lift and fold partially cooked eggs so uncooked portion flows underneath. Continue cooking over medium heat about 4 minutes or till eggs are cooked throughout but are still glossy and moist. Remove from heat.
4 eggs	
¼ cup milk	
4 slices thin-sliced ham, cut into bite-size pieces	

4 croissants, split Thousand Island salad dressing	● Spread top halves of croissants with some salad dressing. Sprinkle cheese over bottom halves. Spoon egg mixture onto cheese-topped croissants. Add croissant tops. Makes 4 servings.
½ cup shredded cheddar, Monterey Jack, *or* Swiss cheese (2 ounces)	

It doesn't take an egghead to recognize a good food deal. This hot sandwich goes together fast and tastes great, too. Serve it with hot cooked peas and fruit for a no-fuss meal.

Eggs 'n' Taters

Total Time: 20 minutes

Pictured on pages 20 and 21.

¼ cup cooking oil	● In a 10-inch skillet heat cooking oil over medium heat. Carefully add frozen potatoes. Cook about 8 minutes or till potatoes are done, turning occasionally. Drain on paper towels.
½ of a 16-ounce package frozen fried potato nuggets	

6 eggs	● Drain all but about 1 tablespoon of oil from skillet. In a mixing bowl beat together the eggs, milk, and oregano.
⅓ cup milk	
¼ teaspoon dried oregano, crushed	

½ cup shredded cheddar cheese (2 ounces)	● Add egg mixture to skillet. Cook, without stirring, over medium heat till mixture begins to set on bottom and around edges. Using a large spoon or spatula, lift and fold partially cooked eggs so uncooked portion flows underneath. Sprinkle cooked potatoes over eggs. Continue cooking over medium heat for 2 to 3 minutes or till eggs are cooked throughout but are still glossy and moist. Remove from heat and sprinkle with cheese. Makes 4 servings.

The kids cleaned their plates when they sampled this dish. They said they'd eat it for breakfast, lunch, or dinner.

Egg-in-a-Bundle

Pictured on pages 20 and 21.

Total Time: 35 minutes

2 **eggs**	● Preheat the oven to 400°. In a small saucepan cover eggs with warm water. Bring to boiling. Reduce heat. Cover and simmer for 15 minutes. Pour off water. Fill saucepan with cold water. Add ice cubes and let eggs cool for 2 minutes. Shell and halve the cooked eggs.
1 **package (8) refrigerated crescent rolls** 4 **1-ounce slices American cheese** 2 **tablespoons cooked bacon pieces**	● Meanwhile, press seams of crescent rolls together to make 4 rectangles. Cut cheese slices in half lengthwise. Place 2 halves on each rectangle, overlapping in the center. Sprinkle with bacon pieces.
Milk **Caraway, poppy,** *or* **sesame seed** 4 **strawberries, sliced (optional)** 4 **orange wedges (optional)**	● Place *one* egg half on the short end of each rectangle. Roll up dough around egg, cheese, and bacon. Pinch sides to seal well. Brush each bundle with some milk. Sprinkle with desired seed. Bake in the 400° oven for 12 to 14 minutes or till golden brown. Garnish with strawberries and orange wedges, if desired. Makes 4 servings.

Save even more time with hard-cooked eggs purchased at a deli. Or, cook eggs ahead and store them for up to one week in your refrigerator.

You'll-Love-It Quiche

Total Time: 35 minutes

Nonstick spray coating *or* **shortening** 1½ **cups milk** 4 **eggs** ¼ **cup all-purpose flour** 2 **tablespoons toasted wheat germ** *or* **cornmeal** ¼ **teaspoon onion powder**	● Preheat the oven to 400°. Spray a 9-inch pie plate or quiche pan with nonstick spray coating, or grease with shortening. In a blender container combine milk, eggs, flour, toasted wheat germ or cornmeal, and onion powder. Cover and blend mixture for 15 seconds.
¾ **cup shredded Monterey Jack cheese (3 ounces)** ¼ **cup grated Parmesan cheese** 2 **tablespoons cooked bacon pieces**	● Pour into prepared plate or pan. Sprinkle with Monterey Jack cheese, Parmesan cheese, and bacon pieces.
	● Bake in the 400° oven for 18 to 20 minutes or till a knife inserted near the center comes out clean. Let stand for 5 minutes. Makes 4 servings.

I LOVE THIS

Buy already cooked bacon pieces at your supermarket. Or try purchased cooked ham or pepperoni pieces.

EXTRA FAST

Total Time: 15 minutes

Fajita Pitas

¾ **pound beef flank** *or*
   sirloin steak
1 **tablespoon cooking oil**
½ **of a green pepper,**
   coarsely chopped
2 **tablespoons Italian salad**
   dressing

● Cut steak into bite-size strips. Preheat a 12-inch skillet over medium-high heat. Add cooking oil. Stir-fry meat and green pepper for 2 to 3 minutes or till meat is done. Remove from heat. Drain if necessary. Toss with salad dressing.

Fajita Pitas were a hit with our young food experts. "I could eat two of these," said Mitch, one of our tasters.

2 **large pitas, halved**
   crosswise
½ **of a 4-ounce package**
   (½ cup) shredded
   cheddar cheese
   Salsa *or* **taco sauce**

● Fill each pita half with some of the meat mixture. Top with cheese. Serve with salsa or taco sauce. Serves 4.

Tabletop Kids' Art

Kid-made place mats can make dinner more fun.
● For the base of a simple place mat, use stiff paper such as construction paper or poster board. First, cut it into a rectangle or even some fancier shape, such as a heart or an oval.
● Next, turn your young artist loose on the base with crayons or felt-tip markers. Or, let your budding Picasso cut out shapes from colored construction paper, tissue paper, or origami paper and glue the shapes onto the base with rubber cement.
● For the finishing touch, seal the artwork between sheets of clear adhesive-backed vinyl. It'll last longer and wipe clean after each meal.

Supermarket Timesavers

Dinner for the family in just minutes. Too good to be true? Not if you team our Last-Minute Meals main dishes with a side dish from your supermarket. The deli section, freezer case, and grocery shelves are loaded with timesaving accompaniments.

Match our Pan-Style Taco on page 10 with canned fruit topped with flavored yogurt, for example. Or, serve the Broiled Peanut Butter Sandwich on page 18 with prepared canned soup and an apple. Or, try the Applesauce Meat Ring on page 44 with baked refrigerated breadsticks and a tossed salad from the supermarket salad bar.

The combinations are endless. Here's a list of supermarket products to start you thinking. Next time you shop, take notes on what's available at your store.

From the Produce Department
Already-cut-up fresh vegetables
Serve-yourself salad bar
Unpeeled fresh fruit

From the Shelves
Quick-cooking rice mixes
Quick-cooking brown rice
Quick-cooking long grain and wild rice mixes
Quick-cooking pasta mixes
Quick-cooking potato mixes
Instant grits
Canned rice mixes
Flavored gelatin
Canned cut-up fruit
Canned cut-up vegetables
Fruit sauces
Breadsticks
Muffin mixes
Brown-and-serve rolls
Canned soups
Dry soup mixes
Crackers
Cake mixes
Pudding mixes
Ready-to-serve puddings
Cheesecake mixes
Cookie and brownie mixes
Cookies

From the Freezer Case
Vegetables with cream or cheese sauce
Rice with or without vegetables
Muffins and muffin rounds
Croissants
Patty shells
Soups
Stuffing mix
Toasted hash browns
Cheesecakes
Pies
Pastries
Frosted cakes
Pound cake
Ready-to-bake cookies

From the Refrigerator Case
Breadsticks
Biscuits
Crescent rolls
Cinnamon rolls
Bread loaves
Heat-and-serve biscuits
Ready-to-bake cookie doughs

From the Deli
Coleslaw (vinegar-based or creamy)
Fruit salads
Gelatin salads
Hot vegetables
Pasta salads
Hot vegetables
Puddings and other desserts

From the Bakery
Bagels
English muffins
Quick breads and muffins
French bread
Dinner rolls
Cakes
Cookies
Pastries
Pies

Quick-Fix Combinations Made from Purchased Parts
Fruit-flavored gelatin made with canned fruit chunks
Canned fruit mixed with fruit-flavored yogurt
Off-the-shelf breadsticks dipped in process cheese spread
Fruit-flavored soft-style cream cheese spread on quick breads or muffins
Canned pie filling in an already-made crumb pie shell
Pudding over sliced or cubed cake

Egg-and-Salmon-Salad Sandwiches

Total Time: 30 minutes

4 **eggs**	● To hard-cook eggs, place them in a small saucepan and cover with cold water. Bring to boiling. Reduce heat to just below simmering. Cover and cook for 15 minutes. Run cold water over eggs to cool. Remove shells. Coarsely chop eggs.
1 **6½-ounce can boneless, skinless salmon, drained and flaked** ¼ **cup cream-style cottage cheese** ¼ **cup coarsely chopped walnuts** 2 **tablespoons sweet pickle relish** 2 **tablespoons mayonnaise *or* salad dressing**	● In a medium mixing bowl combine eggs, salmon, cottage cheese, walnuts, pickle relish, and mayonnaise or salad dressing. Toss to combine.
3 **small pitas *or* 8 slices wheat bread** **Lettuce leaves**	● Spoon ¼ *cup* salad mixture in each lettuce-lined pita. (Or, sandwich the salad mixture with lettuce between 2 slices of bread.) Makes 4 servings.

Chill the canned salmon and cook the eggs ahead. That way, the sandwiches will take only half the time to make and the filling will be chilled.

Total Time: 15 minutes

Salmon Burgers

1 **beaten egg** ½ **cup herb-seasoned stuffing mix** 1 **12½-ounce can boneless, skinless salmon, drained and flaked**	● In a medium mixing bowl stir together egg and stuffing mix. Add drained salmon and mix well. Shape into four ½-inch-thick patties.
1 **tablespoon cooking oil** 4 **cheese slices**	● In a large skillet cook patties in hot oil over medium heat for 2 to 3 minutes or till brown. Carefully turn and cook about 2 minutes more or till brown. Top with cheese slices. Remove skillet from heat. Let cheese melt over burgers.
4 **hamburger buns** **Lettuce leaves (optional)** **Tomato slices (optional)** **Tartar sauce, cocktail sauce, *or* catsup**	● Serve each patty on a hamburger bun with lettuce and tomato, if desired. Top with tartar sauce, cocktail sauce, or catsup. Makes 4 servings.

Canned salmon now comes already boned and skinned to save you time.

Home-Style Meatball Stew

Total Time: 25 minutes

2 cups water
1 10¾-ounce can condensed vegetable soup
1 cup frozen mixed vegetables
½ teaspoon Italian seasoning
1 ounce tiny shell macaroni (¼ cup)

● In a large saucepan combine water, vegetable soup, mixed vegetables, and Italian seasoning. Bring to boiling. Add uncooked shell macaroni and cook, covered, for 5 minutes.

There's no precooking the meatballs for this stew. Just let them simmer till done in the broth.

1 pound ground raw turkey
Shredded cheddar *or* Swiss cheese (optional)

● Drop the meat by spoonfuls into the sauce mixture (or, form meat into ¾-inch balls.) Return to boiling. Reduce heat. Cover and simmer for 12 to 14 minutes or till meatballs are done and macaroni is just tender. Top each serving with cheese, if desired. Serves 4.

Snappy Chicken Stir-Fry

Total Time: 20 minutes

1 6-ounce package frozen pea pods
2 boned skinless chicken breasts (about 1 pound)
¼ cup orange juice
2 tablespoons water
2 tablespoons soy sauce
2 teaspoons cornstarch

● Let pea pods stand at room temperature to partially thaw. Meanwhile, cut chicken into 1-inch pieces. In a small bowl stir together the orange juice, water, soy sauce, and cornstarch.

Use quick-cooking rice and let it stand while you stir-fry the chicken.

1 tablespoon cooking oil

● Preheat a wok or large skillet over high heat. Add cooking oil. Stir-fry chicken, half at a time, for 2 to 3 minutes or till done. Add more oil as necessary. Return all chicken to wok. Push chicken to the sides of the wok. Add orange juice mixture to center of wok. Cook and stir till orange juice mixture is thickened and bubbly.

Hot cooked rice
½ cup peanuts

● Add partially frozen pea pods to wok and stir in chicken till all is coated with sauce. Cover and simmer the mixture for 1 minute. Serve with rice. Sprinkle with peanuts. Makes 4 servings.

EXTRA FAST

Total Time: 15 minutes

Stacked Chicken Salad Sandwich

4 6-inch flour tortillas	
½ cup soft-style cream cheese	
1 cup deli chicken *or* tuna salad	
3 leaves iceberg lettuce	

● Spread *three* tortillas with cream cheese. Top each with some chicken or tuna salad, then a lettuce leaf. Stack tortillas; top with remaining tortilla.

We've taken kid-favorite sandwich ingredients and put them in a new sandwich shape. Top each wedge with a decorative toothpick for fun.

3 to 4 pimiento-stuffed olives, pitted ripe olives, gherkins, *or* cherry tomatoes (optional)

● Cut stack into wedges to serve. Pierce each wedge with a decorative pick or a toothpick topped with olives, gherkins, or tomatoes, if desired. Makes 3 servings.

Baked Parmesan Chicken

Total Time: 40 minutes

4 boned skinless chicken breast halves (about 1 pound)	● Preheat the oven to 375°. Rinse chicken and pat dry with paper towels.
½ cup cornflake crumbs 2 tablespoons grated Parmesan cheese ¼ teaspoon Italian seasoning 3 tablespoons margarine *or* butter, melted	● In a bowl combine cornflake crumbs, Parmesan cheese, and Italian seasoning. Dip chicken pieces in melted margarine or butter, then roll in cornflake mixture. Place on a baking rack in a shallow baking pan. Bake in the 375° oven about 30 minutes or till done. Serves 4.

While the chicken bakes, put together the rest of the meal. Our suggestions: a fruit salad and hard rolls.

Nacho Chicken Pot Pie

Total Time: 35 minutes

½ of a 15-ounce package folded refrigerated unbaked piecrust 1 11-ounce can condensed nacho cheese *or* cheddar cheese soup 1 cup frozen peas ½ cup water 1 3-ounce package cream cheese with chives, cut up	● Set piecrust out at room temperature. Preheat the oven to 450°. In a large saucepan combine soup, frozen peas, water, and cream cheese. Cook and stir over medium-high heat till bubbly.
2 5-ounce cans chunk-style chicken ½ cup quick-cooking rice	● Gently stir in *undrained* chicken and uncooked rice. Return to boiling. Pour into a 1½-quart casserole.
	● Top with piecrust. Trim to ½ inch beyond edge of casserole. Fold under pastry and flute edge. Cut slits in crust to allow steam to escape. Bake in the 450° oven for 15 to 20 minutes or till crust is golden. Makes 4 servings.

If your children like the hot spiciness of Mexican food, use the nacho cheese soup option. Kid-taster Jim endorsed the dish: "I want my Mom to make this tonight. Can I have some more?"

One-Pot Turkey Spaghetti

Total Time: 25 minutes

2 cups water 1 15½-ounce jar spaghetti sauce 4 ounces spaghetti, broken up (about 1 cup)	● In a large saucepan stir together water and spaghetti sauce. Bring to boiling. Add broken spaghetti and cook, covered, for 10 minutes.
1 pound fully cooked smoked link turkey sausage *or* frankfurters, halved lengthwise and sliced into bite-size pieces 1 medium zucchini, halved lengthwise and sliced	● Add turkey and zucchini to pan. Return to boiling. Reduce heat. Cover and simmer about 5 minutes or till spaghetti is just tender and mixture is heated through.
Grated Parmesan cheese	● Sprinkle Parmesan cheese over each serving. Makes 4 servings.

Here's the easiest spaghetti recipe you'll ever cook. The spaghetti simmers in the sauce instead of cooking separately in water.

Little Chicken Dippers

Total Time: 25 minutes

1 12-ounce package frozen breaded small chunk-shape chicken patties	● Preheat the oven to 400°. Arrange frozen chicken on a shallow baking sheet. Bake in 400° oven for 10 to 12 minutes or till chicken patties are done.
¼ cup bottled barbecue sauce 2 tablespoons grape jelly	● For dipping sauce, in a small saucepan heat together barbecue sauce and grape jelly just till the jelly melts.
	Serve warm dipping sauce with chicken. Makes 3 or 4 servings.

The spicy dipping sauce complements frankfurters and fish, too.

Pick Your Pizza

What did our kid tasters choose as their favorite food? Pizza! Then they proved it. They gobbled up *every* form of pizza here: topping on a traditional crust, topping on halved French bread, and topping on flour tortillas. Then they scooped up turnovers made with a pizza filling. We decided pizza was a winner. We think your family will agree.

Personal Pizza
(see recipe, page 36)

French-Bread Turkey Pizzas
(see recipe, page 34)

Ham and Cheese Pizza
(see recipe, page 34)

"Say, Cheese" Calzone
(see recipe, page 35)

Total Time: 15 minutes

French-Bread Turkey Pizzas

Pictured on page 32.

2 6- to 8-inch-long French rolls	● Preheat the broiler. Halve French bread lengthwise. Hollow out each half, leaving a ½-inch-thick shell.
8 ounces fully cooked smoked link turkey sausage, chopped 1 8-ounce can pizza sauce ½ cup frozen diced green pepper 1 4-ounce package (1 cup) shredded mozzarella cheese	● In a medium saucepan stir together the turkey sausage, pizza sauce, and green pepper. Heat through. 　Meanwhile, on an ungreased baking sheet place bread halves, cut side up. Sprinkle *half* of the cheese atop bread halves. Spoon turkey mixture into bread halves. Sprinkle with remaining cheese.
	● Broil 4 to 5 inches from the heat for 2 to 3 minutes more or till cheese is melted. Serve immediately. Serves 4.

Pizza without the work! Halved French rolls form ready-made crusts for single-serving pizzas.

Ham and Cheese Pizza

Total Time: 20 minutes

Pictured on page 33.

2 6-inch flour tortillas 1 cup shredded Swiss cheese (4 ounces) 2 1-ounce slices cooked ham, chicken, *or* turkey, cut into bite-size strips ½ of a small tomato, coarsely chopped	● Preheat the oven to 400°. Place tortillas on a baking sheet. Sprinkle tortillas with *half* of the cheese and all of the meat. Sprinkle tomato atop. Sprinkle with remaining cheese.
Bottled barbecue sauce, taco sauce, *or* catsup (optional)	● Bake in the 400° oven for 8 to 10 minutes or till cheese melts and pizza is heated through. Cut into wedges or fold in half to eat. Drizzle with sauce or catsup, if desired. Makes 2 servings.

Need to serve four? Double the recipe and bake the pizzas in two shifts, serving each person a half-pizza while the other pizzas bake.

"Say, Cheese" Calzone

Total Time: 35 minutes

Pictured on pages 32 and 33.

Nonstick spray coating
or **shortening**
1 **10-ounce package refrigerated pizza dough**

● Preheat the oven to 400°. Line a 12-inch pizza pan with foil and spray with nonstick spray coating, or grease with shortening. Press dough onto foil in pan, forming a 12-inch circle.

Save yourself some cleanup time by covering the pizza pan with foil. The foil also makes the dough easier to fold over the filling.

---

1 **cup shredded cheddar cheese**
1 **cup shredded mozzarella cheese**
½ **cup ricotta cheese**
¼ **cup grated Parmesan cheese**

● In a large mixing bowl stir together cheeses. Spoon cheese mixture on ½ of the pizza dough. Fold dough over filling to form a half-circle (see photo, below). Seal edges, then use the edge of a spoon to make a decorative edge, if desired. Cut slits for escape of steam.

---

1 **cup thick-style spaghetti sauce** *or* **one 8-ounce can pizza sauce**

● Bake in the 400° oven for 18 to 20 minutes or till filling is heated through and cheese is melted. Cover with foil after 10 minutes of baking to prevent overbrowning. Cool on pan on a wire rack for 5 minutes before serving.

　　Meanwhile, in a small saucepan heat spaghetti or pizza sauce. Serve the sauce with calzone. Makes 4 servings.

Place the filling on half of the dough. Fold the remaining dough over the filling and seal the edges with your fingers. Add a decorative edge to the dough using the tip of a spoon, if you like.

Personal Pizza

Total Time: 35 minutes

Pictured on page 4 and on pages 32 and 33.

Personalize the pizza for a special occasion. Write on the baked pie using catsup, taco sauce, or other toppings.

1 **10-ounce package refrigerated pizza crust**	● Preheat the oven to 425°. Press dough into a greased 13x9x2-inch baking pan. Build up edges of crust slightly.
Taco Pizza, Cheeseburger Pizza, *or* Italian-Style Pizza ingredients	● Choose 1 of the pizza flavors below. In a skillet brown the ground meat. Drain off fat. Place about *three-fourths* of the cheese over the crust. Pour the sauce over the cheese. (If desired, reserve some of the sauce to drizzle over finished pizza.) Sprinkle with cooked meat, then sprinkle the remaining cheese over meat.
	● Bake in the 425° oven for 15 to 20 minutes or till crust is done. Sprinkle with taco chips, pickle, or olives and reserved sauce, if desired. Serves 4 to 6.

TACO PIZZA

1 **pound ground raw turkey**
8 **ounces sliced Monterey Jack cheese**
1 **cup taco sauce**
¾ **cup coarsely crushed taco chips**

CHEESEBURGER PIZZA

1 **pound ground beef**
8 **ounces sliced cheddar cheese**
1 **8-ounce can tomato sauce**
½ **cup chopped dill pickle *or* pickle relish**

ITALIAN-STYLE PIZZA

1 **pound bulk Italian sausage**
8 **ounces sliced mozzarella cheese**
1 **8-ounce can pizza sauce**
½ **cup chopped ripe olives**

Smiling Pineapple Salads

EXTRA FAST

Total Time: 15 minutes

1 cup cream-style cottage
   cheese
2 tablespoons raisins

● Divide cottage cheese among 4 salad plates. Using the back of a spoon, spread cottage cheese to form 4-inch circles. Sprinkle with raisins.

1 8¼-ounce can pineapple
   slices, drained
   Raisins, maraschino
   cherries, carrot,
   coconut, dried fruit,
   banana, chow mein
   noodles, *and/or* nuts

● Place a pineapple slice atop each circle of cottage cheese for the face. Choose from raisins, maraschino cherries, banana, chow mein noodles, carrot, coconut, dried fruit, and/or nuts to make the face. Makes 4 servings.

Let your child have fun fashioning a face on each pineapple salad, while you finish preparing the rest of the meal.

"More, Please" Broccoli And Rice

Total Time: 15 minutes

1 **10-ounce package frozen broccoli cuts** 1 **cup quick-cooking rice** 1 **cup water**	● In a medium saucepan combine frozen broccoli, uncooked rice, and water. Bring to boiling, stirring occasionally to break up frozen broccoli.
1 **4-ounce package (1 cup) shredded cheddar *or* Swiss cheese**	● Remove from heat. Cover and let stand for 5 minutes. Over low heat, stir in cheddar or Swiss cheese just till cheese melts. Makes 4 to 6 servings.

Introduce your kids to broccoli with this cheesy recipe. If they're already broccoli buffs, it'll disappear even faster.

Honey-Cream Fruit

Total Time: 5 minutes

½ **cup soft-style cream cheese** 2 **tablespoons honey** ½ **cup cherry *or* orange yogurt**	● In a small mixing bowl stir together the cream cheese and honey till smooth. Stir in cherry or orange yogurt.
Canned unpeeled apricot halves, fruits for salad, peach slices, *or* pear slices	● Spoon desired fruit into individual dishes. Dollop about *2 tablespoons* cream cheese mixture atop each serving. Store remaining topping, covered, in the refrigerator for up to 1 week. Stir before serving. Makes 1 cup.

Quick-chill canned fruit in the freezer for 15 minutes before serving. If you can spare the time, cut up fresh fruit.

EXTRA FAST

Total Time: 15 minutes

Fast Cheese Sticks

⅓	cup mayonnaise *or* salad dressing
¼	cup grated Parmesan cheese
½	teaspoon Italian seasoning

● Preheat the broiler. In a small bowl stir together mayonnaise, Parmesan cheese, and Italian seasoning.

When the kids are hungry NOW, take their minds off their hunger and get some help by having them spread the cheese mixture on the buns.

| 3 | hot dog buns, split |

● Spread *1 tablespoon* mayonnaise mixture on cut side of each bun half. Bias-cut each in half crosswise.

● Arrange on a baking sheet. Broil 3 to 4 inches from heat for 2 to 3 minutes or till golden. Makes 3 or 4 servings.

Total Time: 20 minutes

Wheat-Flecked Biscuits

	Nonstick spray coating *or* shortening
1	cup packaged biscuit mix
¼	cup whole wheat flour
2	tablespoons sunflower nuts (optional)
½	cup plain yogurt

● Preheat the oven to 450°. Spray a baking sheet with nonstick spray coating or grease with shortening. In a mixing bowl combine biscuit mix, whole wheat flour, and sunflower nuts, if desired. Stir in yogurt just till mixture is moistened.

Our kid tasters recommended slathering these biscuits with jam, jelly, or peanut butter. Serve the biscuits with cocoa for breakfast, with soup for lunch, or with about anything for dinner.

● Drop dough by spoonfuls onto prepared baking sheet. Bake in the 450° oven for 8 to 10 minutes or till golden. Makes about 8 biscuits.

EXTRA FAST

Total Time: 15 minutes

Nachos for Dinner!

¾ **pound ground beef** ⅓ **cup taco sauce**	● In a 1½-quart microwave-safe casserole crumble ground beef. Micro-cook, covered, on 100% power (high) for 4 to 6 minutes or till meat is brown, stirring once. Drain fat. Stir in taco sauce.	**The nacho lovers in your family will agree with Jeff. "I'd eat these nachos for lunch, dinner, and breakfast," he said.**
4 cups tortilla chips **2 cups shredded cheddar** *or* **Monterey Jack cheese (8 ounces)**	● On each of 2 microwave-safe dinner plates layer *half* of the tortilla chips, meat mixture, and cheese. Cook each plate on high for 1½ to 2½ minutes or till cheese melts. Cook the second plate of nachos while you serve the first.	
Dairy sour cream (optional) **Chopped tomatoes (optional)** **Sliced ripe olives (optional)**	● Serve with sour cream, tomatoes, and olives, if desired. Serves 4.	

Conventional Directions: Preheat the broiler. In a small skillet brown ground beef. Drain fat and stir in taco sauce.

On a pizza pan layer all of the chips, meat mixture, and cheese. Broil 4 to 5 inches from the heat for 2 to 3 minutes or till cheese melts. Serve as directed.

Attention, Microwave Owners

The recipes in *Fast-Fixin' Kids' Recipes* with microwave directions were tested in countertop microwave ovens that provide 600 to 700 watts of cooking power. The microwave cooking times are approximate because microwave ovens vary by manufacturer.

Dill Potatoes And Sausage

Total Time: 20 minutes

2 medium potatoes (about 12 ounces total) **2 tablespoons water**	● Scrub potatoes. Trim ends. Cut potatoes into ¼-inch-thick slices. In a microwave-safe 1½-quart casserole combine potatoes and water. Micro-cook, covered, on 100% power (high) for 7 to 10 minutes or till potatoes are tender, stirring twice.
⅓ cup mushroom _or_ onion gravy **¼ cup dairy sour cream _or_ yogurt** **⅛ teaspoon dried dillweed** **8 ounces fully cooked smoked sausage links, sliced, _or_ one 8-ounce fully cooked ham slice, cut into cubes**	● In a small bowl combine gravy, sour cream or yogurt, and dillweed. In the casserole gently stir sausage or ham and gravy mixture into the potatoes. Cook on high for 2 to 4 minutes or till heated through. Makes 4 servings.

Here's a hot main-dish potato salad our tasters quickly polished off.

Crunch-Top Tuna Casserole

Total Time: 20 minutes

1 9-ounce package frozen green beans **¼ cup water**	● In a microwave-safe 1½-quart casserole combine frozen beans and water. Micro-cook, covered, on 100% power (high) for 3 to 5 minutes or just till beans are crisp-tender, stirring once.
1 10¾-ounce can condensed cream of potato soup **1 6½-ounce can tuna _or_ boneless skinless pink salmon, drained and flaked** **¾ cup quick-cooking rice** **¾ cup water** **½ cup shredded cheddar cheese (2 ounces)** **½ cup dairy sour cream** **½ teaspoon Worcestershire sauce**	● Stir in condensed soup, tuna or salmon, uncooked rice, water, cheddar cheese, sour cream, and Worcestershire sauce. Cook, covered, on high for 6 to 8 minutes or till bubbly, stirring twice. Let stand, covered, for 5 minutes.
1 2.8-ounce can French-fried onions	● Sprinkle French-fried onions around the edge. Cook, uncovered, for 1 minute more. Makes 4 servings.

Crunchy French-fried onions make an instant topping for this creamy casserole. Serve fruit for dessert, and your meal is complete.

Total Time: 10 minutes

Curly Chili Dogs

1	7½- to 8-ounce can chili with beans
2	tablespoons bottled barbecue sauce
1	teaspoon prepared mustard

● In a microwave-safe 1-quart casserole combine *undrained* chili with beans, barbecue sauce, and mustard.

The secret is in the slice. Four small slits in each frank allow it to curl as the meat cooks.

| 4 | frankfurters |

● Make 4 small slits crosswise in each frankfurter, cutting to, but not through, the opposite side. Stir into bean mixture in the casserole.

| 4 | hamburger buns *or* hot dog buns, split |

● Cover and micro-cook on 100% power (high) for 4 to 5 minutes or till mixture is heated through and frankfurters curl, stirring once. Place curled frankfurters on hamburger buns or uncurl and place on hot dog buns. Spoon chili mixture atop. Serves 4.

Sausage-Corn Chowder

Total Time: 20 minutes

12	ounces fully cooked link smoked turkey sausage *or* frankfurters
1	10¾-ounce can condensed cream of potato soup
1⅓	cups milk (one soup can)
1	8¾-ounce can cream-style corn
2	*or* 3 slices American cheese, torn in pieces (2 or 3 ounces)

● Halve sausage or frankfurters lengthwise and slice ½ inch thick. Set aside. In a microwave-safe 2-quart casserole combine condensed soup, milk, and corn. Stir in turkey sausage or frankfurters and cheese. Micro-cook, covered, on 100% power (high) 7 to 10 minutes or till heated, stirring once.

No sausage or frankfurters on hand? Omit the meat and serve the corn chowder with a sandwich for a hearty lunch or light supper.

| | Croutons (optional) |

● Serve hot chowder topped with croutons, if desired. Makes 4 servings.

Applesauce Meat Ring

Total Time: 20 minutes

1 beaten egg
¼ cup herb-seasoned
     stuffing mix, crushed
¼ cup applesauce
¼ teaspoon salt
1 pound lean ground beef
     or ground raw turkey

● In a medium mixing bowl combine the egg, stuffing mix, applesauce, and salt. Add meat and mix well.
　In a 9-inch microwave-safe pie plate shape meat mixture into a 6-inch ring, 2 inches wide (see photo, below).

On a scale of 1 to 10, our kid tasters gave this recipe a thumbs-up rating—10.

● Cover meat ring with waxed paper. Micro-cook meat on 100% power (high) for 7 to 9 minutes or till no pink remains, giving the dish a half-turn after 4 minutes. Let cooked meat ring stand, covered, for 5 minutes.

½ cup applesauce

● Meanwhile, in a 1-cup microwave-safe measure cook applesauce, uncovered, on high for 1 to 1½ minutes or till heated through. Transfer ring to a platter. Serve with applesauce. Makes 4 servings.

To ensure even cooking, shape the meat mixture into a ring that's 6 inches in diameter and 2 inches wide. Our cooking time is based on this shape.

EXTRA FAST

Total Time: 15 minutes

Tasty Taco Salad

¾ **pound ground beef** *or* **ground raw turkey** 1 **to 2 teaspoons chili powder**	● In a 1-quart microwave-safe casserole crumble ground beef or turkey. Sprinkle with chili powder. Micro-cook, covered, on 100% power (high) for 3½ to 4½ minutes or till no pink remains, stirring once. Drain fat.
1 **8-ounce can tomato sauce** 1 **8-ounce can kidney beans, drained**	● Stir in tomato sauce and beans. Cook, covered, for 2 to 3 minutes more or till heated through, stirring once.
6 **cups torn iceberg lettuce** 4 **tortilla bowls** *or* **4 cups broken tortilla chips** 1 **cup shredded cheddar cheese (4 ounces)** **Dairy sour cream (optional)** **Taco sauce (optional)**	● To serve, arrange lettuce in tortilla bowls or over broken chips. Top with hot meat mixture. Sprinkle with cheddar cheese. Add sour cream and taco sauce, if desired. Serves 4.

Look for ready-to-serve tortilla bowls in your grocer's deli section.

Barbecue-Sauced Chicken

Total Time: 25 minutes

2 **pounds meaty chicken pieces**	● Rinse chicken and pat dry. In a 12x7½x2-inch baking dish arrange chicken pieces, skin side down, with the meaty portions toward the edges of the dish. Cover with waxed paper. Micro-cook on 100% power (high) for 12 to 15 minutes or till no pink remains. After 8 minutes, give the dish a half-turn, turn pieces skin side up, and rearrange, putting cooked portions toward the center. Drain fat from chicken.
¼ **cup bottled barbecue sauce** ¼ **cup catsup** ½ **cup shredded mozzarella cheese (2 ounces)**	● Combine barbecue sauce and catsup. Spoon over chicken, brushing to coat pieces. Cook, uncovered, on high for 1 to 2 minutes or till heated through. Sprinkle with cheese. Cook for 1 minute more. Makes 4 to 6 servings.

To reduce fat, skin the chicken. Then cook, covered, with vented microwave-safe clear plastic wrap instead of waxed paper.

Total Time: 15 minutes

Micro Burger

Also pictured on the cover.

¼ **cup creamy Parmesan *or* creamy Italian salad dressing**
¼ **cup fine dry bread crumbs**
1 **pound ground beef**

● In a medium mixing bowl combine salad dressing and bread crumbs.
    Add ground beef and mix well. Shape into four ¾-inch-thick patties. Arrange in an 8x8x2-inch baking dish. Cover dish with waxed paper.

● Micro-cook on 100% power (high) for 6 to 8 minutes or till no pink remains. After 3 minutes, drain fat. At the same time, give the dish a half-turn and turn the meat patties over.

4 **hamburger buns, split**
  Lettuce
  Catsup, mustard, pickles, *and/or* sliced tomatoes

● Toast buns. Serve patties on buns with lettuce and condiments. Makes 4 servings.

Have a burger picnic in your own backyard without heating up the grill or your house. Your burgers will cook in the microwave oven in just 8 minutes.

Micro Spud and Toppers

Total Time: 25 minutes

4 medium potatoes (6 to 8 ounces each)	● Scrub potatoes and prick skins with the tines of a fork. On a microwave-safe plate arrange potatoes, spoke fashion.
	● Micro-cook potatoes on 100% power (high) for 14 to 17 minutes or till tender, rearranging once. Let stand 5 minutes.
Thousand Island Topper, Hot Cheese Topper, or Broccoli Topper	● Meanwhile, prepare topper. Cut a slit in the top of each potato. Press on ends to open slit. Spoon some topping over each potato. Makes 4 side-dish servings.
	Thousand Island Topper: Stir together ½ cup *dairy sour cream* and 2 tablespoons *Thousand Island salad dressing.* Makes ⅔ cup.
	Hot Cheese Topper: In a microwave-safe 2-cup measure place ½ of a 5-ounce jar *cheese spread* (about ¼ cup). Micro-cook, uncovered, on 100% power (high) for ½ to 1½ minutes or till cheese is melted, stirring to blend. Stir in ¼ cup *dairy sour cream.* Cook for 30 seconds more, stirring once. Spoon over potatoes. Drizzle with 2 tablespoons *salsa,* if desired. Makes ¾ cup.
	Broccoli Topper: In a microwave-safe 1-quart casserole micro-cook 1 cup loose-pack cut *broccoli* and 1 tablespoon *water* for 3 to 4 minutes or till tender. Cut up any large pieces. Stir in ½ of an 8-ounce container *soft-style cream cheese* and ½ teaspoon *Worcestershire sauce.* Cook, covered, on 100% power (high) for 1 to 2 minutes or till heated through. Makes ¾ cup.

Your microwave oven cooks potatoes in about a quarter the time of your conventional oven.

Creamy French-Fry Casserole

EXTRA FAST

Total Time: 15 minutes

1 7¾-ounce can semicondensed tomato soup ¼ cup shredded cheddar cheese ½ teaspoon Italian seasoning *or* dried basil, crushed	● In a microwave-safe 1½-quart casserole combine tomato soup, cheddar cheese, and Italian seasoning. Micro-cook, covered, on 100% power (high) for 2 to 3 minutes or till cheese melts, stirring mixture every minute.
3 cups frozen loose-pack French-fried potatoes ¼ cup shredded cheddar cheese	● Fold in frozen potatoes. Cook, covered, on high for 6 to 8 minutes or till mixture is heated through. Sprinkle with shredded cheddar cheese. Makes 4 or 5 side-dish servings.

Kid taster Peter said the casserole tasted like two of his favorites—spaghetti sauce and French fries.

Extra-Easy Haystacks

Total Time: 20 minutes

½ cup semisweet chocolate pieces 2 1.8-ounce packages chocolate-covered peanut butter cups	● In a microwave-safe 1½-quart casserole combine chocolate pieces and peanut butter cups. Micro-cook on 100% power (high) about 2½ minutes, stirring after 1½ minutes. Stir till nearly smooth.
1 3-ounce can chow mein noodles ½ cup peanuts	● Stir in noodles and peanuts till coated.
	● Drop by rounded tablespoonfuls onto a baking sheet lined with waxed paper. Quick-chill in the freezer about 8 minutes or till firm. Store, covered, in the refrigerator. Makes 20 cookies.

Chocolate-covered crunch best describes this microwave sweet. Instead of peanuts, try cashews, raisins, or dried fruit bits.

Blueberry-Apple Crisp

Total Time: 30 minutes

2 **tablespoons brown sugar**
1 **tablespoon all-purpose flour**
1 **20-ounce can sliced apples, drained**
2 **cups frozen blueberries *or* unsweetened pitted tart red cherries**

● In a small bowl stir together brown sugar and flour. In a microwave-safe 1½-quart casserole toss together apples, frozen fruit, and brown sugar mixture. Micro-cook, covered, on 100% power (high) for 5 to 7 minutes or till hot, stirring fruit twice.

½ **cup quick-cooking rolled oats**
¼ **cup packed brown sugar**
¼ **cup all-purpose flour**
1 **teaspoon apple pie spice *or* pumpkin pie spice**
3 **tablespoons margarine *or* butter**

● Meanwhile, in a medium mixing bowl stir together the oats, brown sugar, flour, and spice. Cut in the margarine or butter till the mixture resembles coarse crumbs. Sprinkle the crumb mixture over fruit.

Light cream *or* ice cream (optional)

● Cook, uncovered, on high for 4 minutes. Let stand for 10 minutes. Serve warm with cream or ice cream, if desired. Makes 6 servings.

Pick your fruit—blueberry or cherry—for this fresh-tasting treat. Assemble the crisp before dinner, then cook it while you eat your meal.

Shortcut Spices

You'll find we've used spice blends often in *Fast-Fixin' Kids' Recipes*. Why? Because they save you the chore and the time of measuring multiple herbs or spices. The seasoning section of your supermarket is brimming with choices. Italian seasoning, five-spice powder, pizza seasoning, and poultry seasoning are a few you can use to perk up savory foods. For sweets, try apple pie spice and pumpkin pie spice.

Total Time: 5 minutes

Peanut butter (optional)
1 **plain rice cake**
½ **of a 1- to 1½-ounce bar milk chocolate**
12 **tiny marshmallows**

Rice Cake S'mores

● If desired, spread peanut butter on rice cake. On a microwave-safe plate top rice cake with chocolate, then marshmallows. Do not cover. Micro-cook on 100% power (high) for 18 to 20 seconds. Let stand for 30 to 60 seconds. Makes 1 serving.

Minty Rice Cake S'more: Prepare as directed, *except* substitute 2 cream-filled chocolate-covered *peppermint patties* for the milk chocolate.

S'mores are as much fun to make as they are to eat. The kids can watch the marshmallows puff in the microwave. For a more traditional s'more, substitute 2 graham cracker squares for the rice cake.

Whirl a blender beverage that's ready to serve in less than 10 minutes. Pour ingredients into the blender container, then let the kids work the blender—they'll enjoy being at the controls. Pour a tall drink for breakfast, lunch, after-school treat, dinner, or snack. When the kids aren't looking, whip one up for yourself.

Total Time: 5 minutes

Yoguberry Fizz

1 **8-ounce carton pineapple, lemon, peach,** *or* **vanilla yogurt**	● In a blender container or food processor bowl combine yogurt, frozen berries, and apricot nectar. Cover and blend till smooth. Pour into 4 tall glasses.
1 **cup frozen loose-pack berries**	
½ **cup apricot nectar**	
1 **12-ounce can chilled ginger ale** *or* **lemon-lime carbonated beverage**	● Add ginger ale or lemon-lime beverage to glasses. Stir and serve immediately. Makes 4 (8-ounce) servings.

Mix and match your child's favorite frozen berries and flavor of yogurt. If you like, sieve the blended mixture when using raspberries. Then, stir in the ginger ale.

Total Time: 10 minutes

Razzle-Dazzle Lemonade

1½ **cups cold water**	● In a blender container combine water and frozen lemonade or orange juice concentrate. Cover and blend smooth. Stir in lemon-lime beverage.
1 **6-ounce can frozen lemonade** *or* **orange juice concentrate**	
1 **16-ounce bottle lemon-lime carbonated beverage**	
4 **scoops lemon** *or* **orange sherbet**	● Place a scoop of sherbet in each of 4 tall glasses. Pour lemonade mixture over the sherbet. Top each with a strawberry. Makes 4 (12-ounce) servings.
Fresh *or* **loose-pack frozen strawberries**	

Here's an after-school pick-me-up to keep your hungry kids happy until dinner.

Total Time: 5 minutes

Goin' Bananas Malt

1 pint chocolate *or* vanilla ice cream
1 small ripe banana, cut up
½ cup milk
¼ cup instant malted milk powder

● In a blender container combine ice cream, banana, milk, and malted milk powder. Cover and blend till smooth.

For a chillier malt, freeze the cut-up banana before blending it.

● Pour blended malt into tall glasses. Makes 3 (8-ounce) servings.

Total Time: 10 minutes

Swashbuckler's Island Slush

1 8¼-ounce can crushed pineapple
1 6-ounce can frozen pineapple *or* orange juice concentrate
¼ cup cream of coconut
3 cups ice cubes

● In a blender container combine *undrained* pineapple, frozen juice concentrate, and cream of coconut. Cover and blend till smooth. With blender running, add ice cubes, 1 at a time, through opening in lid. Blend till the pineapple mixture is slushy.

Our kid tasters slurped this slush right down. "It tastes just like a frozen pineapple," agreed Amanda and Julie.

1 12-ounce can chilled grapefruit carbonated beverage

● Add carbonated beverage to container and stir gently. Pour into glasses. Makes 6 or 7 (6-ounce) servings.

Self-Cleaning Blender

Your blender saves you time while it whips up drinks; now let it save you time by cleaning itself. Fill the blender container about one-fourth full with warm water, then add some dishwashing liquid. Cover and blend. Swish the blender lid with some of the soapy water to clean. Rinse the container and lid with hot water. Invert, and let dry in the dish drainer.

Blender Beverage Blitz

Here you see 10 refreshing thirst quenchers. Some start with juice, some with milk or ice cream, and others with canned or frozen fruit. Each will tame a growling tummy.

Blend together 1 cup milk and 3 tablespoons chocolate ice cream topping. Serves 1.

Blend together ½ of a 6-ounce can (⅓ cup) frozen grape juice concentrate and one 12-ounce can ginger ale or club soda. Blend in 6 ice cubes, one at a time, to form a slush. Serves 2.

Blend together one 8-ounce carton peach yogurt and one 8¾-ounce can peaches, drained. Add 6 to 8 ice cubes, one at a time, blending to form a slush. Serves 3.

Blend together one 10-ounce package frozen strawberries, one 6-ounce can apricot nectar, and 2 to 3 tablespoons cold water. Serves 2 or 3.

Blend together one 8-ounce carton cherry-vanilla yogurt, 1 tablespoon dry instant eggnog, and ½ cup milk. Add 2 ice cubes and blend. Serves 2.

Blend together 1 cup chocolate ice cream and ½ cup milk. Add 1 chocolate sandwich cookie and blend till coarsely crushed. Serves 2.

Blend together 1 drained 11-ounce can mandarin orange sections, 1 cup orange sherbet, and ½ cup orange juice. Add 4 to 6 ice cubes, one at a time, blending to form a slush. Serves 3.

Blend together 1 cup ice cream, ¼ cup milk, and 2 tablespoons peanut butter. Serves 1 or 2.

Blend together ½ cup canned blueberry, cherry, or peach pie filling and 1 cup vanilla ice cream. Serves 2.

Blend together ½ of a 6-ounce can frozen pineapple juice concentrate, 1 cup vanilla ice cream, and 2 to 4 tablespoons milk or water. Serves 2.

Total Time: 10 minutes

Breadstick Snacks

1 **8-ounce container soft-style cream cheese** ½ **cup shredded cheddar cheese (2 ounces)** 2 **tablespoons milk** ½ **teaspoon curry powder *or* chili powder**	● In a medium mixing bowl combine cream cheese, cheddar, milk, and curry or chili powder. Beat till well mixed.
Breadsticks	● Dip breadsticks into cheese mixture. Store any remaining cheese mixture, covered, in the refrigerator for up to 3 days. Makes 1¼ cups dip.

Another time, spread the spicy cheese mixture on apple slices.

Total Time: 5 minutes

Serve-Yourself Rice Cakes

4 **rice cakes *or* graham crackers** **Spiced Peanut Butter Spread *or* Cream Cheese-Apricot Spread**	● Spread each rice cake with about *2 tablespoons* desired spread. Store leftover spread, covered, in the refrigerator for up to 3 days. Makes 4 snack-size servings.
	Spiced Peanut Butter Spread: Stir together ¼ cup vanilla *yogurt,* ¼ cup *peanut butter,* and a dash ground *allspice* till smooth. Makes ½ cup.
	Cream Cheese-Apricot Spread: Stir together ⅓ cup soft-style *cream cheese* and 2 tablespoons *apricot preserves.* Makes ½ cup spread.

For added fun and flavor, top the spread and rice cakes with sliced banana, raisins, or sliced apple.

Stir-In Yogurt Snack

EXTRA FAST

Your child is bound to like at least one of these 5-minute yogurt combinations. Try one the next time you need a quick hunger-stopper. For each snack, stir together the ingredients listed.

Snack No. 1
½ cup strawberry yogurt
2 tablespoons round sweetened
  bran cereal
1 tablespoon toasted coconut

Snack No. 2
½ cup orange yogurt
2 tablespoons raisins
1 tablespoon miniature
  semisweet chocolate pieces

Snack No. 3
½ cup vanilla yogurt
2 tablespoons granola
1 tablespoon peanut butter

Snack No. 4
½ cup lemon yogurt
¼ cup frozen blueberries
1 tablespoon sliced almonds

Snack No. 5
½ cup raspberry yogurt
¼ cup canned fruit chunks,
  drained
1 tablespoon Grape-Nuts cereal

Snack No. 6
½ cup peach yogurt
½ of a small banana, sliced
1 tablespoon sunflower nuts

EXTRA FAST

Total Time: 15 minutes

Crunchy Banana Boats

1 **medium banana**
Fruit flavored soft-style cream cheese *or* peanut butter

● Halve banana lengthwise. Spread 1 cut side with some cream cheese or peanut butter.

Kid tasters Travis and Lisa liked this snack the best of all the recipes they tasted.

Granola

● Press some granola into the cheese. Top with the other banana half. Cut filled banana in half crosswise. Makes 1 or 2 servings.

For Braces Only

Do you have a smile at your house
that's covered with metal? If so,
these three snacks are for you.
They're designed just for kids with
braces on their teeth. Each recipe
is guaranteed friendly to braces.
What's more, plain smiles will like
the snacks, too.

No-Nuts Cereal Snack

Total Time: 35 minutes

2 cups unsweetened puffed corn cereal
2 cups round toasted oat cereal
1 cup small fish-shape cheese crackers
1 cup chow mein noodles
3 tablespoons cooking oil
1 tablespoon dry buttermilk salad dressing mix

● Preheat the oven to 350°. In a 13x9x2-inch baking pan combine cereals, cheese crackers, and chow mein noodles.
Drizzle oil over cereal mixture and toss. Sprinkle with dry dressing mix and toss to coat. Bake in the 350° oven about 10 minutes, stirring once. Cool in pan for 15 minutes. Store in a tightly covered container at room temperature for up to 1 week. Makes 6 servings.

Get some help. Let your child stir together the cereal mixture.

Soft Cheese Nachos

Total Time: 20 minutes

4 6-inch flour tortillas

● Preheat the oven to 450°. Stack tortillas and cut into 4 wedges. On a 12-inch pizza pan arrange tortillas in a single layer, overlapping slightly if necessary. Bake in the 450° oven for 7 to 9 minutes or just till brown.

Crisp corn tortilla chips can wreak havoc on kids' braces. With these nifty nachos based on softer flour tortillas, your child's teeth are safe.

½ cup shredded Monterey Jack cheese (2 ounces)
½ cup shredded cheddar cheese (2 ounces)

● Sprinkle cheeses over tortillas on pan. Return to oven about 2 minutes more or till cheeses melt.

Salsa *or* taco sauce
Dairy sour cream (optional)

● Drizzle with salsa or taco sauce. Dollop with sour cream, if desired. Makes 3 to 4 snack servings.

EXTRA FAST

Total Time: 10 minutes

Cracker Pizzas

12 wheat crackers
1 1½-ounce slice Mozzarella cheese
¼ cup pizza sauce
Sliced pitted ripe olives (optional)

● Preheat the broiler. Arrange crackers in a shallow baking pan lightly sprayed with nonstick spray coating or lightly greased with shortening. Cut cheese slice in half lengthwise and into sixths crosswise, making 12 squares.
Place a piece of cheese on each cracker. Spoon about *1 teaspoon* pizza sauce atop. Top with olive, if desired. Broil 5 to 6 inches from the heat for 1 to 2 minutes or till cheese is melted. Makes 3 or 4 snack servings.

There's no need to heat up your kitchen. Just pop these snacks into your toaster oven. We didn't micro-cook the snacks because they soften too much.

Peanut-Packed Munch Mix

Total Time: 30 minutes

5	cups bite-size shredded wheat biscuits
1	cup unsalted peanuts

● Preheat oven to 350°. In a 13x9x2-inch baking pan combine shredded wheat biscuits and peanuts. Set aside.

¼	cup creamy peanut butter
2	tablespoons margarine *or* butter
1	tablespoon honey

● In a small saucepan heat together peanut butter, margarine or butter, and honey. Drizzle over cereal mixture, tossing to coat.

½	cup raisins

● Bake in the 350° oven about 10 minutes, stirring twice. Cool in pan on a wire rack about 10 minutes. Stir in raisins. Store in a tightly covered container at room temperature for up to 1 week. Makes 8 cups.

Our kid tasters *loved* peanut butter. This snack is doubly delicious with peanuts and peanut butter. One taster, Ingrid, said it was like eating cereal without milk.

Dive-In Caramel Corn

Total Time: 25 minutes

3 tablespoons margarine *or* butter	● Preheat the oven to 325°. In a small saucepan melt margarine or butter. Remove from heat. Stir in corn syrup and molasses.
¼ cup corn syrup	
1 tablespoon molasses	
6 cups popped popcorn	● In a 13x9x2-inch baking pan drizzle molasses-syrup mixture over popcorn, tossing to coat.
1 cup dry roasted peanuts cashews *or* sunflower nuts	● Bake in the 325° oven about 15 minutes, stirring twice. Transfer mixture to a serving bowl. Stir in peanuts. Store in a tightly covered container at room temperature. Makes about 4 cups.

Stand back when you set this crunchy snack in front of your kids. They're likely to dive in for a handful of this treat.

"Thank You For The Great Food," proclaims the colorful banner drawn for us by this smiling group of kid tasters.

EXTRA FAST

Total Time: 10 minutes

Good-Night Cocoa

2½ cups nonfat dry milk
      powder
1½ cups tiny marshmallows
 1 cup sifted powdered sugar
 ½ cup powdered nondairy
      creamer
 ½ cup unsweetened cocoa
      powder

● In a storage container combine milk powder, marshmallows, powdered sugar, dry creamer, and cocoa powder. Tightly cover and store at room temperature for up to 3 months. Makes 4¾ cups.

Boiling water

● For *each* serving, combine ⅓ *cup* mix with ¾ *cup* boiling water.

Rich Good-Night Cocoa: Prepare mix as directed, *except* stir in 1 cup *instant eggnog mix.* Sprinkle each serving with ground *nutmeg,* if desired.

Good-Night Cinnamon Cocoa: Prepare mix as directed above, *except* stir in 1 tablespoon ground *cinnamon.*

Minty Good-Night Cocoa: Prepare mix as directed above, *except* stir in ½ cup *butter mints,* crushed.

Hot cocoa warms the heart and soothes the soul. That's why it's great for kids *and* their parents. Add extra marshmallows as the others melt. Or, top with whipped cream or a small scoop of ice cream.

On the next six pages you'll find breakfast recipes that go together faster than it takes the coffee to perk. For those mornings you want to sleep in, look for the make-ahead recipes your kids can serve themselves while you snooze.

Toaster French Toast

Total Time: 30 minutes

⅔ cup milk
2 eggs

● In a shallow dish beat together the milk and eggs.

8 slices apple-cinnamon
    bread *or* cinnamon-
    raisin bread
Cooking oil

● Dip both sides of bread in beaten mixture. Let stand till well moistened. On a griddle or in a large skillet cook bread in hot oil over medium-high heat about 2 minutes per side or till golden.

Margarine *or* butter
    (optional)
Maple-flavored syrup
    (optional)

● Cool on waxed paper. Place in a tightly covered container and store in the refrigerator. To serve, toast in the toaster. Serve with margarine or butter and syrup, if desired. Makes 4 servings.

Our kid tasters liked this French toast plain—no margarine or syrup. Freeze cooked French toast in a freezer container. Then toast twice in the toaster to heat through.

EXTRA FAST

Total Time: 10 minutes

Eye-Opener Spread

⅔ cup peanut butter
⅓ cup soft-style cream
    cheese
2 tablespoons honey

● Stir together the peanut butter, soft-style cream cheese, and honey.

¼ cup raisins
¼ cup coconut
Toasted English muffins,
    wheat toast, *or* toasted
    frozen waffles

● Stir in raisins and coconut. Store, covered, in the refrigerator up to 1 week. To serve, spread on English muffins, wheat toast, or waffles. Makes 1⅓ cups.

If your kids aren't crazy about coconut, substitute shredded carrot.

Jumbo Peanut Butter Scones

Total Time: 25 minutes

½ cup vanilla yogurt 2 tablespoons peanut butter 1¼ cups packaged biscuit mix	● Preheat the oven to 400°. In a medium bowl stir together the yogurt and peanut butter. Stir in the baking mix.
2 to 3 teaspoons sugar	● On a baking sheet pat dough with floured fingers to form a 5-inch circle about ¾ inch thick. Cut into 6 wedges. Sprinkle with sugar.
	● Bake in the 400° oven about 15 minutes or till light brown. Serve warm. Makes 6 scones.

Jelly, jam, or honey make natural toppers for this breakfast biscuit.

Oven-Baked Pancakes

Total Time: 20 minutes

2 cups packaged pancake mix 1½ cups milk 1 egg 2 tablespoons cooking oil ½ teaspoon ground cinnamon	● Preheat the oven to 425°. In a medium mixing bowl stir together pancake mix, milk, egg, cooking oil, and cinnamon. (Batter will have small lumps.)
½ cup fresh blueberries, ¼ cup miniature semisweet chocolate pieces, *or* 2 tablespoons cooked bacon pieces	● Stir in the blueberries, chocolate pieces, or bacon. Pour into a greased 15½x10½x1-inch baking pan.
Maple-flavored syrup Margarine *or* butter (optional)	● Bake in the 425° oven about 10 minutes or till done. Cut into squares. Serve with syrup and margarine or butter, if desired. Makes 6 squares.

You also can use frozen blueberries—just thaw them under running water for a minute or two.

1 To form the snails, coil one breadstick as shown above.

2 Wrap another breadstick around the first coil to form a larger snail shape.

3 Place the coiled breadsticks on the sugared surface, then roll to ⅛-inch thickness.

Cinnamon Snails

Total Time: 25 minutes

	Nonstick spray coating
3	tablespoons sugar
½	teaspoon ground cinnamon
¼	cup finely chopped nuts

1	package (8) refrigerated breadsticks

● Preheat the oven to 375°. Spray a baking sheet with nonstick spray coating. Combine sugar, cinnamon, and nuts. Sprinkle sugar mixture on rolling surface.

● Unroll 1 breadstick. Coil tightly. Wrap another breadstick around coil, forming a larger coil. Place on sugared surface. Roll to ⅛-inch thickness.

Place sugared side up on baking sheet. Repeat with the remaining 6 breadsticks. Bake in the 375° oven about 15 minutes or till golden. Serve warm. Makes 4 servings.

For an easier-to-eat version, make Soft Cinnamon Snails: prepare recipe as directed, *except* on a baking sheet use four breadsticks to form each of two coils. Brush with melted margarine. Sprinkle with sugar mixture. Bake in a 350° oven for 18 to 20 minutes. Serve warm. Serves 4.

Whiz-Bang Banana Muffins

Total Time: 45 minutes

1 cup all-purpose flour
½ cup quick-cooking
    oatmeal
¼ cup packed brown sugar
1 tablespoon baking powder
½ teaspoon ground
    cinnamon
⅛ teaspoon salt
    Nonstick spray coating
    or shortening
	● Preheat the oven to 400°. In a large mixing bowl stir together the flour, oatmeal, brown sugar, baking powder, cinnamon, and salt. Set aside. Spray muffin pan with nonstick spray coating or grease with shortening.

⅓ cup milk 1 egg 2 tablespoons cooking oil	● In a blender container combine milk, egg, and oil. Cover and blend smooth.
1 large ripe banana	● With blender running, cut up banana and blend into mixture. Pour into dry ingredients and stir just till moistened. Fill muffin pans ⅔ full. Bake in the 400° oven about 20 minutes or till done. Makes 10 to 12.

The whizzing blender speeds up the mixing process. If you don't have a blender, just beat together the milk, egg and cooking oil and mash the banana by hand.
Freeze any extra muffins. Keep them on hand for a fast breakfast.

EXTRA FAST

Total Time: 5 minutes

Cream-Cheese Super Spread

1 8-ounce container soft-
    style cream cheese
¼ cup orange marmalade
¼ cup chopped pecans *or*
    walnuts
	● In a tightly covered container combine cream cheese, orange marmalade, and nuts. Cover and store spread in the refrigerator for up to 1 week.

Split bagels *or* English muffins, toasted	● To serve, spread on bagels or English muffins. Makes 1¼ cups spread.

This bread spread mixes up in minutes, then you can dip into it for breakfast all week long.

EXTRA FAST

Total Time: 15 minutes

Sugar 'n' Spice Bagels

¼	cup sugar
1	teaspoon ground cinnamon
¼	teaspoon dried orange peel (optional)
⅛	teaspoon ground nutmeg

● Combine sugar, cinnamon, orange peel, and nutmeg. Store in a tightly covered container. Makes about ¼ cup sugar and spice mixture.

Sprinkle the sugar mixture on buttered toast, waffles, or pancakes, too.

4	bagels, split and toasted Strawberry, pineapple, *or* plain soft-style cream cheese

● Spread cut side of bagels with a thin layer of cream cheese. Sprinkle with some of the sugar and spice. Serve warm. Makes 4 servings.

Honey-Raisin Refrigerator Muffins

Total Time: 45 minutes

2	cups all-purpose flour
2	teaspoons baking powder
1	teaspoon pumpkin pie spice *or* apple pie spice

● In a large mixing bowl stir together flour, baking powder, and spice. Make a well in the center.

Muffins any time you want them! This batter can wait in your refrigerator for as long as one week.

2	beaten eggs
½	cup packed brown sugar
½	cup cooking oil
½	cup milk
⅓	cup honey
1	cup raisins

● Combine eggs, brown sugar, oil, milk, and honey. Add all at once to dry ingredients, stirring just till moistened. Fold in raisins.
　　Transfer batter to a tightly covered container. Cover and store in the refrigerator for up to 1 week.

● To serve, line muffin cups with paper bake cups or grease with shortening. Without stirring batter, fill muffin cups ⅔ full. Bake in a 350° oven about 25 minutes or till done. Makes 14 to 16.

Microwave directions: Prepare and store batter as directed above. To serve, line microwave-safe 6-ounce custard cups or microwave-safe muffin pan with paper bake cups. Fill ⅔ full with batter. Micro-cook, uncovered, on 100% power (high) for 30 to 60 seconds for 1 muffin, for 1 to 2 minutes for 2 muffins, for 1½ to 2½ minutes for 4 muffins, and 2 to 3 minutes for 6 muffins, turning once.

Celebrate big and small successes with a special treat. Choose from pie, brownie pizza, ice cream, cookies, or cake. What a way to mark your child's first day of school, that A in geometry, or a birthday! Pages 74 and 75 are packed with quick decorations you assemble in just minutes.

One-Bear Salute

Total Time: 40 minutes

1 20-ounce roll refrigerated chocolate chip cookie dough

● Preheat the oven to 350°. Cut the cookie roll crosswise into thirds. On the bottom half of a large baking sheet pat 1 portion into a 6-inch circle to form the body. Pat another portion of dough to form another 6-inch circle for head, pressing circles together at neck to seal.

Our Goldilocks gave the giant cookie bear her stamp of approval. "It sure beats eating porridge or taking a nap," she confided.

● Cut the remaining dough into 6 portions. Arrange and pat to form 2 ears and 4 paws.
   Bake in the 350° oven for 13 to 15 minutes or till done. Cool for 2 minutes on baking sheet. Transfer to a serving plate. Cool about 30 minutes before spreading with pudding mixture.

1 4½- to 5-ounce can chocolate pudding
¼ cup cherry-vanilla *or* vanilla yogurt
⅓ cup coconut
   Assorted candies

● Meanwhile, stir together pudding and yogurt.* Cover and chill till ready to serve. Spread over bear body to about 1 inch from the edges. Sprinkle with coconut. Use candies to decorate as desired. Store any leftovers, covered, in the refrigerator. Makes 16 to 20 servings.

*Note: Top with ⅔ cup canned frosting instead of pudding mixture, if desired. Then you can store leftovers, covered, at room temperature.

Three-Cheers Parfaits

Total Time: 20 minutes

¾ cup coarsely crushed cinnamon *or* plain graham crackers
1 8-ounce carton vanilla yogurt
1 4½- to 5-ounce container vanilla pudding

● In 4 individual parfait glasses sprinkle ¼ cup crushed graham crackers. In a small mixing bowl stir together *half* of the vanilla yogurt and the vanilla pudding. Spoon into parfaits.

Hip, hip, hooray! Cheer your child on by rewarding him or her with a tall parfait.

1 4½- to 5-ounce container chocolate fudge pudding

● Sprinkle *¼ cup* more graham crackers over the parfaits. In the same mixing bowl, stir together remaining yogurt and chocolate fudge pudding. Spoon into parfaits. Sprinkle remaining cracker crumbs atop. Serve immediately or cover and refrigerate the parfaits till serving time.

Pressurized whipped dessert topping
4 small decorative cookies *or* maraschino cherries

● To serve, top each parfait with dessert topping and a cookie or maraschino cherry. Makes 4 servings.

Total Time: 15 minutes

A Week of Sundaes

⅓ cup semisweet chocolate pieces
½ cup *sweetened condensed milk*

● For hot fudge sauce, in a small saucepan melt together the semisweet chocolate pieces and the sweetened condensed milk.

There are so many flavors of ice cream, preserves, and toppings, you could have a different sundae every day of the week. Keep any leftover fudge sauce, covered, in the refrigerator. To serve, reheat in a small saucepan over low heat.

4 purchased brownies (optional)
Vanilla, strawberry, *or* chocolate ice cream
Strawberry preserves, cherry preserves, *or* orange marmalade

● Break up brownies and place in 4 individual dessert dishes, if desired. Top with ice cream. Spoon hot fudge sauce over ice cream. Dollop about *1 teaspoon* preserves or marmalade over each.

Pressurized whipped dessert topping
Coarsely broken pretzels, coarsely chopped peanuts, *or* pecans

● Top with whipped dessert topping. Sprinkle with pretzels, peanuts, or pecans. Makes 4 servings.

Rocky-Road Brownie Pizza

Total Time: 40 minutes

Nonstick spray coating *or* **shortening** 1 **roll refrigerated brownie dough**	● Preheat the oven to 350°. Spray a 12-inch pizza pan with nonstick spray coating or grease with shortening. Spread dough over bottom of pan.
	● Bake in the 350° oven for 25 to 30 minutes or till done. Cool in pan on a wire rack for 10 minutes. Transfer to a serving plate.
½ **of a 7-ounce jar marshmallow cream** ⅓ **cup chopped nuts** ⅓ **cup miniature semisweet chocolate pieces**	● Immediately dollop with marshmallow cream. Let stand for 1 minute to soften, then spread evenly. Sprinkle with chopped nuts and chocolate pieces. Cut into wedges to serve. Serve warm or cool. Makes 16 to 20 servings.

Place any leftover pizza in the freezer, uncovered, for 30 minutes. Then, cover with moisture- and vaporproof wrap and freeze. To serve, let the pizza stand at room temperature for 15 to 20 minutes.

EXTRA FAST

Pint-Size Peanut Butter Pie

Total Time: 15 minutes

½ **of an 8-ounce package cream cheese, cut up** ¼ **cup peanut butter** 2 **tablespoons sifted powdered sugar** 1 **tablespoon milk**	● In a mixer bowl beat together cream cheese and peanut butter till well blended. Add powdered sugar and milk. Beat mixture well.
½ **of a 4-ounce container frozen whipped dessert topping, thawed** ⅓ **cup coarsely chopped peanuts**	● Fold in thawed whipped dessert topping, then chopped peanuts.
4 **graham cracker tart shells** **Desired ice cream topping** *or* **fresh fruit (optional)**	● Spoon mixture into individual tart shells. If desired, chill in the freezer for up to 20 minutes before serving. Drizzle with ice cream topping or top with fresh fruit, if desired. Makes 4 servings.

When you come home from the supermarket, store the whipped dessert topping in your refrigerator so it will be thawed when you need to use it. The topping will keep for up to 2 weeks.

Cake and Cookie Smiles

Everyone will be smiling when you and your child put together these festive treats. Best of all, they're as easy as pressing candy into frosting. Look at these ideas to begin, then let your imagination guide you.

Start with a base of frosted or unfrosted cakes, cupcakes, cookies, or doughnuts. Then add decorations—candies, cereal, fruit, small cookies, sprinkles, coconut, or semisweet chocolate pieces. Use canned or decorator tubes of frosting as "glue."

Is it your turn to make the treats? Don't worry, help is at hand. Choose from any of these six recipes designed just for the occasion. They're easy to make, they travel well, and kids love them.

Because most treats arrive at their destination in your child's hands, pack them so they'll hold up under some jostling. Start with a tightly covered container and gently pack some crumpled waxed paper on top to keep them from bouncing.

Fudgy Brownie Cupcakes

Total Time: 35 minutes

1 cup sugar ½ cup margarine *or* butter 4 eggs	● Preheat the oven to 350°. Line muffin pans with paper bake cups. Set aside. In a large mixer bowl beat sugar and margarine till fluffy. Beat in the eggs.
1 16-ounce can (1½ cups) chocolate-flavored syrup 1¼ cups all-purpose flour ¾ cup miniature semisweet chocolate pieces	● Stir in syrup, then flour. Stir in chocolate pieces. Fill muffin cups ½ full with chocolate cupcake batter.
⅓ cup chopped walnuts	● Sprinkle walnuts over the tops of the unbaked cupcakes. Bake in the 350° oven for 18 to 20 minutes. Cool in pans on wire racks. Makes 24 cupcakes.

These rich cupcakes use not one but two kinds of chocolate. Your family chocoholics will be proud to tote them to their next function.

EXTRA FAST

So-Simple Treats

Total Time: 5 minutes

1 16-ounce package candy-coated milk chocolate pieces 3 cups dry roasted peanuts 2 cups raisins 1 cup coconut	● In a large bowl toss together the candy-coated chocolate pieces, peanuts, raisins, and coconut.
	● Using a ⅓-cup measure, scoop the mixture into 24 clear plastic sandwich bags. Tie with a ribbon or colorful pipe cleaner. Makes 24 treats.

This is the simplest treat of all. Let children serve themselves and scoop out a paper-cupful.

Dutch Apple Bars

Total Time: 45 minutes

Nonstick spray coating
or shortening
2¼ cups all-purpose flour
½ cup packed brown sugar
2 teaspoons baking powder
1 teaspoon ground
cinnamon
¼ teaspoon salt

● Preheat the oven to 375°. Spray a 13x9x2-inch baking pan with nonstick spray coating or grease with shortening.
In a large mixing bowl stir together the flour, brown sugar, baking powder, cinnamon, and salt.

Either regular or chunk-style applesauce does the trick for this cakey cookie.

3 eggs
1 8-ounce jar applesauce
(1 cup)
½ cup cooking oil
½ cup coarsely chopped nuts

● In a medium bowl combine eggs, applesauce, and oil. Stir in nuts.

Streusel Topping

● Stir apple mixture into flour mixture till well blended. Pour into prepared pan. Sprinkle with Streusel Topping.
Bake in the 375° oven about 25 minutes or till done. Cool on a wire rack. Cut into rectangles. Makes 24 to 36 bars.

● **Streusel Topping:** In a small mixing bowl combine ½ cup *all-purpose flour* and ¼ cup packed *brown sugar*. Cut in ¼ cup *margarine* or *butter*. Stir in ½ cup coarsely chopped *nuts*.

Candy-Bar Bars

Total Time: 45 minutes

Nonstick spray coating
or shortening
1 2-layer-size package
German *or* milk
chocolate cake mix
1 5-ounce can (⅔ cup)
evaporated milk
⅓ cup margarine *or* butter,
melted
1 cup chopped nuts

● Preheat the oven to 350°. Spray a 13x9x2-inch baking pan with nonstick spray coating or grease with shortening. In a large mixer bowl beat together cake mix, milk, and margarine or butter till well mixed. Stir chopped nuts into the beaten mixture.

Cake mix shortcuts the measuring for this candy-bar-topped bar cookie.

3 2.6-ounce chocolate-
covered peanut-caramel-
nougat bars *or*
6 chocolate-covered
peanut butter cups,
chopped

● Spread *half* of the mixture into prepared pan. Bake in the 350° oven for 10 minutes. Sprinkle with chopped candy. Drop remaining cake mixture by teaspoons over all. Bake about 15 minutes more or till done. Cool on a wire rack. Cut into rectangles. Makes 36.

Easy Peanut Butter Bars

Chewy Granola Goodies

Candy-Bar Bars
(see recipe, page 77)

Easy Peanut Butter Bars

Total Time: 25 minutes

Nonstick spray coating *or* shortening 1 cup packed brown sugar ½ cup peanut butter ¼ cup cooking oil 2 eggs	● Preheat the oven to 350°. Spray a 13x9x2-inch baking pan with nonstick spray coating or grease with some shortening. Set aside. In a large mixing bowl beat together the brown sugar, peanut butter, cooking oil, and eggs till well blended.
¼ cup milk 1½ cups self-rising flour*	● Beat in milk, then beat in flour till well combined. Spread into prepared pan.
¾ cup peanut butter-flavored pieces ½ cup coarsely chopped peanuts	● Sprinkle peanut-butter-flavored pieces and peanuts atop. Bake in 350° oven 20 to 25 minutes or till done. Cool in pan on a wire rack. Cut into bars. Makes 32.
	***Note:** We used self-rising flour because it saves measuring additional ingredients. If you don't keep it on hand, substitute a mixture of 1½ cups *all-purpose flour,* 1 teaspoon *baking powder,* and ½ teaspoon *baking soda.*

Peanut-butter-flavored pieces combine with peanuts for a special topping. This sturdy, frosting-free bar cookie travels well.

Chewy Granola Goodies

Total Time: 20 minutes

1 10-ounce bag regular marshmallows ¼ cup margarine *or* butter	● Line a 13x9x2-inch pan with foil. Butter foil. Set aside. In a large saucepan combine the marshmallows and margarine or butter. Cook and stir mixture till the marshmallows are melted.
4 cups granola with raisins 1½ cups crisp rice cereal ½ cup sunflower nuts	● Stir in granola with raisins, crisp rice cereal, and sunflower nuts.
	● Press mixture into the prepared pan. Cool. Remove foil lining with uncut bars from pan. Cut into bars. Makes 24.

"Terribly delicious" is how kid taster Emily rated this no-bake cookie.

Index